SURVIVAL

TAKES A WILD

IMAGINATION

SURVIVAL
TAKES A WILD
IMAGINATION

Poems

FARIHA RÓISÍN

Andrews McMeel
PUBLISHING®

In Remembrance of Mahasweta Devi:
"I'm being condemned as a witch."

Dedicated to my survival.
I'm proud of you, Fa.

Contents

The beginning, the body, the wound

I.

*"Another world is not only possible, she's on her way. On a quiet day, if you listen
very carefully, you can hear her breathe."* —Arundhati Roy

"Poetry is a political act because it involves telling the truth." —June Jordan

*"When you are standing by an ocean, alone, within the calmness of your spirit.
Be planetary."* —Etel Adnan

Human Life Is Turbulent

I'm not being coy,
ill-mannered, or vile
when I plead,
oddly subservient,
& declare:
I can't see myself.

When your body, as
a child, was
made not to
be yours,
you become
a ball
of neglected
intuition.

To be worthy feels
devastatingly
inaccurate. I'm
a coma of fear
strapped together
in this ghoulish
parade.
Life—& I'm not
a pessimist—
but, *bitch* . . . life!
Is there a salve
to this gloom?

I count the ways
I love myself,
I'm furthest
from zero
I've ever
been.

A body breaks
under a mighty
yawn,
but it's time
to resuscitate.

I'm a Cancer moon,
I need to be fed.
Calling out >
I see who
s t i c k s <
Who leads
with grace? With
open-hearted
compassion?

Never let someone
convince you out
of your needs,
always walk away
from a half-assed
apology.

I'm tired of empty,
unconvincing ploys
of affection.

Imagine what God is like, girl,
then become *it*.

My Body Is an Archive

"Ma. You once told me that memory is a choice. But if you were god, you'd know it's a flood." —Ocean Vuong

Tommy Girl perfume laced
in pencil shavings—a love
letter for the seven-year-old
me. Lusting across
tabletops as I push that
plump clit (formed like symmetrical
peach slices) against
the thrill, the sharp edge.
The first time I
looked at my vagina was at thirty.
Truthfully, I was scared to see
the flesh-laced hair, to be faced
with my undesirability.
I don't fake orgasms as
often as I fake calm.
Cut it out of me, this wound.
Why did nobody save me?
Please, I beg you. I'm tired
of being punished for my
inescapable horniness. I can still
hear my mother's screech, me
at six, sincere, deer-eyed, curious,
hopeful. "Close your legs, who
are you trying to impress?"

To lose the innocence you
were never afforded.
My God, why hath thou
forsaken me?
Did I survive?
Is that why it feels like grief?
When I remember, *if I can
remember*, that's when I
leap   with grief. The
horizontal violence done
barely
feels plausible. But *it* knows.
My body not only keeps the
score, it keeps a tally, too.
I want to scream,
but who will hear me
when I do?

Fariha Róisín

For Every Girl Who Has Had Her Throat Slit Open

For Aarushi Talwar

The sword carried
        by the weak man, a knife
an instrument of petulance,
        lingers, sadistically
with curious misplaced
        aggression.

Man is weak, bro.
        Everybody knows
boys will be boys
        is short for
these fuckers have no
        evolutionary possibility.

Girls just here 2 murder
        & u know what. Like all
men are in a *True Detective*
        cult, but Matthew McConaughey
ain't come 2 deliver
        justice 2 u, hombre.

It spools, it spills
        blood in the cracks
a slice, laid ear to ear.

Black Dahlia. A strange
hallucination to think my body
goes under yours.

Mate, you're no Ted.
But of course his black
eyes stood deranged
in his uncaring
brain. Was he really *that* charming?
Or was he just white?

How predictable.
They are sad DJs,
failed artists, poems
they try to be Asian for. Elliot Rodger
wasn't mad, he was just entitled.
What's *more* egregious?

Here's the thing, *though*
you can pounce around in your violence
all the mindlessness
that becomes you. Fight wars
& do whatever you need to do
to tell yourself you have meaning.

But nothing will salve ego without grace . . .
. . . is it too late or will you evolve already?
*Are you **not** satisfied?*

Find a better way to process
your mortality & shame
. . . & keep us out of it!

Thousands of years of grueling oppression
yet men still think they're smarter
even if they can't stop fighting or fucking
for a second long enough
to take a good look at all this
& find God

in the folds of the Earth.
Not a moment to take one long
exhale & wonder what sublime mystery
that we are all here, *together*
in this shared experience. The wisdom it would take
for men to break the cycle

to end the hubris in superiority,
finding a way back to their hearts enough to retain humility.
If they could only just take all the moments
needed to weep & say thank you,
thank you, for all of this . . .
for a moment longer than a second . . . & mean it.

Paradise, Girl.
She's Hard to Find.

For my good friend Sarah Hagi & her good looking out

Paradise under
your mother's
feet she tells
me, like
all mothers were
created equal
& all children
were loved.

The supple lips
that kiss me
feel hollow of
real love. One
where I'm not left
questioning
// questioning.

What does it
mean to be
loved? Loved
like you really
mean it? They say
paradise.

I can show you
all the places

on my body
that have remained
unloved. Like
the time she used
a forked wire hanger to
strike me, like
a lash. The many times
my body
was just a body
to her. A body *worthy*
of punishment.

I count the ways
I've been loved
by you. But 1, 2, 3
feels futile
next to the hanging
absence of
what a mother
should be.

It's OK, I
tell myself. I'm
a survivor with a
tempting will.
I have no memory
of vast years
of my life. Stranded,
I run. Motherless.

Turns out,
heavy-lidded, never idle,
she was made
& unmade daily,
by my father's stirs.
Never collapsing,
she did what
she thought
wives do—
but forgot,

      to be a mother

in advance. She
wore neglect,
with a gravity;
Allah's penance.

All I longed for
was her love,
she never noticed.
Instead, I became
an immovable
pillar for her misery.

I did my due
diligence—
didn't I?
Like a soldier on
a mission, "Operation
Save Ammu." Say it
to me, God
wasn't I
enough?

It's too late
for more lies.
Oh, but I'm still
hoping. I'm still
hoping. For

       Paradise.

This Is for Everyone Who Had to Make a Family out of Themselves

I learned magic by July,
my spine coiled.
Rest, they said, rest.
Rest? I asked myself,
mouth full of bees.
People like me, sons of
poor people, Marxists,
people who hate money,
we don't have time
to sleep.

To quiet the sounds of
scarcity
I had to learn that
I was abundant
on my own, see.
No parent whispered to me,
soft: *All this could be yours.*

Creator,
I had to believe,
when the only voice I'd ever
heard from my mother
was a tight, booming:
"No."

There is a song
trapped in each
vertebra.
I'm not alone,
but I've felt the
loss of
empty holidays.

Love is like
the time we asked
our Tamil landlord
how he was doing
& his response was:
"I'll ask my wife."

Being unmothered means
love is a guessing game.
A constant negotiation of
tic-tac-toe. I don't
want a love that is toxic.
Hear my prayer,
I want a love that
knows that to love a wild
thing is to let
it be free, & love me
anyway.

I want to be a person
who chooses light, holy
over seduction. God over

money. Listen to me,
I want to be a person
who sings freedom & believes
it. Releases not only
herself—but her family
from the roots
of their suffering.

On Dying

Abbu,
I seek your guiding light
in the universe.
Already mourning
what's to come.
I've thought of you
dying since
the first moment
I knew you were
the only parent
I had. Yesterday
you told me: "I'm not afraid
of Death; what do we have
to fear from Allah,
the most merciful?
But, I'm claustrophobic.
Incinerate me."
What will I do when
you're gone?

All Brown Men Could Be My Father

For my father, forever.
Ameen

Nehru jackets,
with the collar
popped up like a puffin.
Aligarh educated
the revolutionary men
of a modern India;
South Asia
in bloom.

The curious Bangla gyro-truck
owners who speak to me
in broken English,
not knowing my broken
Bangla could absolve
the situation;
too embarrassed
by my own failing tongue,
I stay silent.

The sweet Afghans
lining the mountains in their fur
cherry lips, like Kiarostami's hero,
Sabzian himself, the echo
of the Soviet death chant in the
valleys, in the valleys,
on Manhattan's turf

pulling the F train
with a curve.

Gujrati men driving taxis,
bodies with grace,
they break shield,
& suddenly their skin papery thin,
living & strange, they turn,
paan-soaked teeth,
cigarette lingering like
a shitty air freshener,
they smile, "Where are you
from?"

They ask, but
the land
that I'm from
is no longer mine.
Under water, under siege,
what does it mean
to have a pulse?

The Bangladeshi uncle in Toronto
who spoke to me about
Shakespeare & Victor Hugo,
with an ailing son—
"He has the comprehension of

      a two-year-old,
      but   with the body

of a   twenty-three-year-old

man."

Tears abundant,
living a life, dependent.
I cried all night,
thinking of you, abbu.
Of all the dreams
you said goodbye to.
I'm sorry, I'm sorry,
I'm sorry, abbu.

When I land in
Al Ain, I see them.
Eyes, distant. Longing
incapable of true emotional
expression.
Stranded, in a land that
deems to be Arab is superior,
a land that misuses
the deen, forgets that
the Prophet reminds us
Arabs will eat dates
once again.

In their yellowed
receptacles, these men,
these men, my father,
my father, I see universes
that never collided.

I see the shame
of being (an) unseen
(fortune), an invisible
plight. An absence,
a loss
of meaning.

They've lost it all
in this fight for survival,
skin like heated tobacco.
It hurts to know,
to teach, to hope.

My abbu, my abbu,
you cry for your brethren,
your comrades, for the
Bangladesh you fought for,
but could never return to.
My father,
my father, if I could cut out
my heart to show you
how proud I am
of you, I would. Knowing
you lacked love, too,
knowing it's all
you ever wanted, too.

My jaan, my liver, my heart—
my father,
how lucky I am
that you raised me

on Tagore—
how no good thing is
mine, but yours.

How you taught me about
climate change, Vandana Shiva
& the importance of Islamic
scholarship—*my father, my father,*
you were my first hero
& forever
that shall remain
till the very last day.

What Does It Mean to Shift a Vibration?

Memories that aren't mine,
I think, I think,
seared into the faculties of my brain,
samskara.
Pain has no glory, it's
where the spit trails, sickness,
undone.
Shape-shifting is no easy sport.
I am becoming me, all the mothers
before me, like an incredulous diamond.
Cut from blood I am turning, inward,
an alchemical tour de force,
I am turning to see the
phantom. I let it move
through me.
Move through to an exhalation.
Move through to an exultation.
That is what I chose for my body
in this lifetime.
To be a vessel, a milky way of feeling,
of grueling healing,
so they can be seen, seen—at last.
At last!
For what else do we ever want,
my darling,
than to be seen?

Amar Sonar Bangla

Gold,
like goldenrod. Our
skin like hazelnut,
a Ferrero Rocher. A
patina of an
old halo sits,
waiting to be
acknowledged &
adorned.

I do not know
what it means
to *be* Bangladeshi,
but I want to
learn about
what my grandfather
fought for.

Please.
Child, run for the
tea hills. Child,
hide, hide, *hide.*

No one mourns
four hundred thousand women—
except the women
who remember
violence,
in our bones.

But don't all women,
feel violence,
            in our bones?

In fifty years, tell
me—*tell me*
the truth: Will there
be a Bangladesh to
return to? Or will
we be submerged
underwater?
Shivering in
the bay like
the long-forgotten
unknown, dead?

Who sings lamentations
for *our* bones? Who remembers
our genocide?
Three million people . . .
can you even c o u n t
to three million?
People.
Abbu never let me look
at the bodies,
but his memory
contains them all.

You can't ever forget,
you can't ever escape.
Memory. I live it for you
every day, ammu
abbu, dado, dadi,
chacha, chachee.
Ancestors guide me out
of this heat, let me heal
your
centuries'
worth   of   pain.

It's all clogged in our
arteries, the disease that
exists like a faint specter
looming at every point
of existence, the *jinn*,
haunting, but what is horror
other than trauma?
Burning mothers
don't scare me,
they remind me
of my past.

Ammu, you made me strong.
Blood-curdling, trauma trapped
in each cell, ammu, you prepared me
for this life.
There is strength wrapped around
every molecular composition
that makes up my soul.

I'm unbreakable like a tall banyan's
roots, children suckling at
my tits. Healing means healing
myself first, innit. Can I show
you how far I have come,
without you?

I'm no longer mad that this was my
karma, someone has to break this
centuries-old grief.
It's a privilege to do it for you,
it's a privilege to do it for my people.

Everything I have ever done was to get
closer to you. Even if it was only in
my own mind.
Amar sonar Bangla, ma,
you gave me my life.
Our stories,
our destinies . . . are linked.

Memories Rewritten

I used to think I'd come home from school & instead of banging pots & pans, I'd find your tenderness. Is it so wrong that I just wanted a sweet word from you? You've never asked me how I am, I used to think because Bangla has no construction for maternal love. But that's untrue. In my dreams you hold my hand, & I am not afraid. In my dreams you, me, & apu eat fish & chips by the oceanside, but no one is crying. I don't know what it's like to be normal. I don't know what it's like to be loved. I used to wish you hugged me like you meant it. Like when I was small & alone, pretending it was OK that I had no one to play with, trapped at home with your temper. What is tenderness? I crave it. I used to dream my touch didn't disgust you, & that yours didn't scare me. I used to know the palms of your hands so well because they'd come down on my body so often. I wish I never remembered. I wish I could forget everything. I hate being the body that screams every secret, kept. I am not a tomb. I am a reckoning. But it's lonely here. Nobody believes what happened to me. They don't believe someone whose name means joy could hold such radiating sadness. But I'm holding the microphone to my heart. I've lost everything. But, I guess I never had you. I still believe in a good life. For you, as well. It's OK, I wish I could have saved you, too. But I pray to Allah for an absolution. I found home in a body that was never loved. For generations, I've been thrown back & forth. But, it's enough now. Be still now. In my dreams you ask me how I am. With your eyes you tell me I'm enough.

Manoosh Ki Bolbe?

A stinging strum,
a haunting beat,
the threat of the phrase
against freedom's reach.
Being small requires no
attention, no examination;
an oversimplification of
the perversity of gossip,
an over-identification
of another's limiting belief.
Who cares what they say
sparks an indelible synapse
that leaks into my blood
stream like cyanide. Poison
spoon-fed from birth, so subtle
its only consequence is
a life-shattering psyche split.
What doesn't kill
you makes you stronger
ahó
I'm realer than I've ever been,
less ugly to myself.
To be known by one's own
being is salvation. It is to witness
God's holy project
& surrender on the basin
of your scratched-up knees.
The mud cherishes your resilience,
it asks you to pray, to awaken, like clay.

To be Muslim means to sublimate rage,
into the divine temple, the spiral of
a dervish, the cry of a qawwali,
decolonize jihad, be mighty!
Pull at your *nafs*, face it before it's
too late. I'm miraculous
like a vine of death, the
God compound, ancestor, grandmother,
the sacred purge, datura's spill,
its rays of polyphonic geometry
slicing into the matrix.
Hiding is not an option anymore.
The stop & start, like a pulse,
a growl. I'm becoming. Can't
tell me nothing. I'm who you never
wanted me to be. I'm who you always
wanted to be.
When I dissent, I'm speaking directly
to you. White teeth bare, calcified
into dust, not enough time
to be alive. Too young to die.
I'm taking back my life,
Hanuman's leap.
I'm doing it
for you. I'm doing it for me.

Liberation, pleasure, joy

II.

"If you don't laugh, you don't survive." —Sonia Sanchez

As Sticky as Marmalade

Sometimes I cum so hard, like sticky, gooey marmalade, steeped
in sugar, glazing on a stovetop. The heat rising like a storm, of
flies, of wind, of musk, like maple syrup collected from the sap.
I am
earthen, pulled from salt & body. It's like I'm gathering all my
cream from all corners & crevices of myself to release it like a
cry, a deep-bellied ache. I have come, I have come. I have built
mountains over you.

On Getting Your Body Back

For Mahasweta Devi

I begin to feel its shape,
pool. The ruffles
of my dress
tethered to my skin,
like petals.

I taste salty. I
touch my mouth
to my fingers, then to my
wetness, like salined
Gatorade.
I have made myself
a drink to be consumed
by only the most eager
& worthy.

I look at myself
in the mirror, puckering
like a sexy girl
oughta, lips plump,
an apple red. Fuji,
mountainous. I smack,
smack, my puckered
quivering lips together
& pout.

I desire myself.

It's taken so long
to look in the
shiny mirror
& like what I
see, staring back.

> I remember the first time
> I saw you, Fa—
> hair frazzled,
> deep soul eyes,
> fully embraced
> by Grandmother
> ayahuasca.
>
> Chuck told you
> to see yourself
> & love,
> everything
> & you staggered
> like a queen not knowing
> the direction to her
> throne.
>
> But when you
> finally looked up
> & saw, saw the
> galaxy-shaped mouth,
> eyes like tiny moons,

haphazard gleam
in your eye—ass fat, belly
popping through the vintage
Dries shirt, I saw you,
& you saw me, *too*.

The Kali-like rage, the
Vishnu kindness, sparing.
Pacha Mama, Mother
Earth, you sang—
"My oh my, I'm
beautiful," with
Sally Field enthusiasm.
& you are, you
were.

You're ugly, you're
funny. When you scowl,
you look like a male movie
star. You're dynamic,
some would say "real."

You've let yourself be,
without control.
Baby, you're getting
your body
back.

Fariha Róisín

On Grief

Brooklyn, New York
4/21/2020

Against my throat, my innards blue. Heaviness subsumes me. Like
a cylindrical cube of pure shite. That's what it is. Wrapped around
my bottom half. Lodged in my belly, IBS, I'm suffocating in this
grayish peril of doom. I'm out of my depth here, honey. The ambu-
lance shrill—there goes another one—strides like a death chant. A
bronchial cough, a decided sound, utters before me. The hiss of the
tremulous radiator awakens you, but you're not here. You're not here,
& I'm alone. Alone to smear Marmite on my toast. Sullen, ugly with
comfort, I fear losing you when I've lost so much. But you have, too.
So we grieve. This time apart strengthens my spine, but the miasma
of grief is trapped in a room—tight with no windows. You can't leave
me here, I feel fragile & unkempt. The ghastly sounds of the city that
never sleeps. It knows not how to process dead bodies (at this rate)
in the most developed nation in the world. I lie in limbo, panting for
you. The grief that we're collectively about to face is inestimable. The
distant shape of the city lingers, the sky unblurry, like a song, crisp,
newly minted on the radio. Sauron's eye blinks on top of the Empire
State Building. I close my eyes, we should rest.

Love Poem

After Audre

I'm rolling my tongue
into a U shape, pretending to
move up on you. Suck you
like a mango. Rooted
in you like a slimy
dream come true.

You're so fine I have
to slap myself
silly to just take
a good look at you.
Eat you like a cherry I pop,
guzzle you like a Valentina.

Open-Hearted Lover

The seduction of
impulse has
launched me into
a wild untameable
dance. I'm lit
like a pinball machine,
ready to sway.

I try to laugh it away.
Oh yes,
love, in the time
of toxic globalization,
& quarantine.
But how my heart
beats for you.

Can you see how it
sinks? Imprinting
my soul with your
name? It pounds
like a Richter scale
ten for you, pouring
through
me, like sand.
This feeling, *this
feeling*

Is this love, I've
asked myself, wanting
doubt to ridicule
me. "Will you
just explain it away?"
The mirror, tricks.
But, how can I
explain away you?

I've never felt
the sensation
of wanting to
throw myself
toward somebody,
completely free,
unmoored.
But, with you I
just want to throw
myself. With
clear, diamond
mind eyes.

Not in a daze, in the
summer light, fixed
like the moon.
You make my dreams quiver,
a pulse in trance.
Sanguine with lust, I'm edging
at such great heights
coalescing my courage
to let you in.

It's you, it's
you. I sigh.
I'm a ball of
clay, orbiting
you, a serenade.
Magnetic, maybe?

I know.
We are made
of the same
stardust. Looking
for the right fit.
I didn't even
know I was ready,
but for you? I guess
it's time.

Time Moves Slow

Signs of times
changing. Clocks
like toys—
what is time,
a spiral of
life, a spiral
of wisdom.
Time is a flat circle,
McConaughey smirk;
no beginning, no end.
A sea endless, to be
here. Now. To
be here. Like
time, endless. Misery,
unknown. I'm
walking toward
you, arms open.
No hours, jumping.
Sweet talk has no
guarantee. On you.
I'm smiling.
Time between this
portal
feels forever. You're near.
No, you're not. Now
where did you go?
Baby. Did you know?
I miss you. Can we dance?

Fariha Róisín

Fog in the mirror, sublime.
Baby, did you know? I can
see your outline, a mirage. I
can feel your lick
on my thigh.
Baby, did you know?
I'm here.

A Pandemic Lamentation

After Wisława Szymborska

Bear witness to a silent time
        of reflection, dust-to-dust, death-to-
death calls like an ailing chant

The *adhaan* of the last breath,
        God, are you there?
This tiny eternity made us

collapse capitalism into a blip.
        Humans so greedy, they think
their lives that they lead for no one

will count for something,
        when all that's ever mattered
was how well you loved, & what you

left behind of it.
        Where does this grief go, friend?
Tell me what to do with these

knots that have plucked me sour,
        like aches rippling across
the majesty, sublime like sand dunes.

My body is arched in preparation for you.
        All the easier to take me,
like the rain.

"Remember the sea," I whisper
        as I lick the wetness that's pooled out of you, like a lake.
"Let her come," I beg. "Let her come."

Lisboa

Under the temple of
Graça's hilltops, an
asylum, along the
chlorophyll, green
tree shades. I sit.
Sweeping, angular slopes
like I dream, being in Palestine,
being free.
Drooping with limes, lemons,
& pomegranates,
speaking in Farsi, in
Fado, oceans stretching
across, airborne,
the sky lined
with kites, rising like color blocks
of geometry. To be held
is no small miracle.
Across the crumbling
nation, I pass through
you, hamburgers in Galeto
using Bourdain's template
as a map, Mo's
compass, a traveler's tongue:
Obrigado, pingado, tudo bem?
Through loss, I'm being
fortified. Ecology, landscape,
the Earth's majesty does that.

Ruth Wilson Gilmore lives here
part time. I think of colonial,
I think of abolition.

Black Narcissus

The energies of the sky-stars move like undulating prophets on the seas. The mountain's dubious light pours onto the stillness of the ground's rind. Like Black Narcissus, time stands still. The sun is bright, bold, booming. I can see. I can see the future. Eons move through you, be still my heart. Be still like candied wine. Be still like a singing lark between songs. I love you with no fear of death, I love you across the oceans & seas. The darkness moves up toward me like a steep volcano, but I am awake with your insolence, & your erratic heart. I'm awake with an affection that is pure. Love is always a battle between the spirits, between the mind & jarring emotions, between the struggles of self & mania. I am with you, I smell faint vanilla, the smoke like a cloud, look up, my hand's out, it's out for you to take, my sweet. Take a leap. Catch me, please. Hold me like I'm worth looking at. Black Narcissus, a silent weep. Be gentle with me.

Finding Earth, God

III.

"Don't ever be surprised
to see a rose shoulder up
among the ruins of the house:
This is how we survived."
—Mosab Abu Toha, "A Rose Shoulders Up"

"What needed to change was changed, just as
old things were destroyed – not by time
but by force of human will."
—Rachel Cusk, *Coventry*

An Ode to Baby Fa

After Lucille Clifton

1.

I pick myself up off the floor. I take myself out of the bathtub &
tell myself: "You don't want to die, you want to live." I wish I had
a mother to do that for me, I wish I had a somebody who could let
me rest my head on their lap & say *shh shh, honey, you've had to work
too hard it's OK, rest here, I love you, honey*. My default is to worry about
whether or not I'm easy to love. Too many people have told me
otherwise. But I know I am, I know I am. So I get up. I get up & I
just get the fucking fuck up & I find some peace. I ask myself, Fa,
what do you want? & baby Fa says what she wants & then I look at
her & say *fuck I love you so much how did you survive* & in that moment
I can either break down on my knees & cry for the life I've had or
I can just say *baby Fa you are a goddamn miracle*. I see you! I see you! &
I love you so much. Thank you for surviving, baby Fa, you've done
such a great job. I wouldn't change anything in the world. You're
perfect. I'm so lucky I get to be you.

2.

So it begins. The air is slight & powerful. The wind hits the
tranquil place within me. It's strong & I'm no longer absent. Now,
I'm present with myself. It's holy & mysterious & I know that it's
alive & I'm patient. I know like the sun, like rain, it spools & I'm
pulsing. It's the leaves like the green of pistachio; green like basil—
the Earth is green & so are the trees, & in that aliveness of it all,
rapturous, rapturous, I am still on this Earth . . . I am still.

3.

Who sees you when you come into yourself? When you stretch & make space for all the longing, for all the ugly? Who protects you then?

4.

The hurricane speaks. The lark strings through the sprouting trees & I'm abandoned. But the Earth is here & I am still. Still like the quiet spurring of a cicada, they reach their tenuous sounds while never moving & yet, & yet—resounding.

5.

Today is a rainy day. It's a day that has character. A sort of ruinous character, moving. I anger in silence, alone through devastation, while seeking love like a beggar. I am hungry for it, mother. I am hungry for a love that will feed the void you left inside of me. The void ever-present, a pulse running through me. There is a tempest within me. A longing, an ache, a hunger unpronounced.

6.

I've been waiting, hiding, in prayer, in the motions, pruning in the gardens of hope, edging closer to an understanding of self. There are so many things that make a self, so many considerations & configurations of being, but I've been trapped in darkness for so long. Its memory is ever present, ever possible, trauma is always on the horizon. It takes rewiring to believe in more, it takes courage to hope.

7.

Tragedy needs examination. No one can ever save you from the turmoil of grief. You have to choose wisely in whom to trust when you're on the floor squirming at injustice. But pain also has its resolution; this too shall pass.

8.

So I celebrate the small grand act of making something big out of a life that coulda turned'a tragedy. No one's sympathy will ever be a salve for the permanent feeling of loss. Whose words will help overcome generations of trauma? You can do it, Fa, you can remember yourself.

9.

This life will pass you by in a blip. No cause or concern, then you're gone. Pain can be hypnotic, find joy in the dance. Choose yourself, especially when no one else will. Find magnificence in solitude. Find God again & again.

10.

But mostly, find celebration.

For every day that has tried to kill you . . . & failed.

Blue Crystal Fire

After Robbie Basho

The trees with sparkling grace,
lined with crystal, water gems
stars streaming through
the creek of the branches, the bark
so illuminating.
Receptacles reflecting
the eternal, God,
the sun.

An Ode to Three Sunsets

A psychedelic streak. Pomelo pink, fluro like a highlighter, swirled
like a strawberry candy cane. The vermillion sky swoops in, the
blue dusk, an ash of storm, just like a Turner streak. The cascade
of tangerine, opaque yet glimmering. I fell in love there.

Lime like le rayon vert, comme Éric Rohmer. Chartreuse like the
northern lights. This world is a paradise. I've never seen a stretch
that wide, so expansive. A blue planet in & of itself, the sunset,
an orb. First time I felt whipped & embraced by the sacred water.
Freer than I've ever been in my red swimsuit, *Baywatch*. I'm trying
to love my body's maps, the gorgeous rivulets along my thighs.
I'm close, I can feel her breath on my cheek. Let go.

I watch the waves for mystery, a stranger emerging from the
ocean. The dolphin fin peaks like a crown, edging the water,
along the gentle rim of the horizon, like a marbled orange &
pink iris. I'm scared of the vastness that I see, the crashing of the
waves by my window lurches a somatic response. Who's to tell
you how to be afraid? Use the tapping motion, EMDR, Dorothy
with her red shoes. Maybe Kansas was always here. Home is no
mirage. I'm safe.

Deep Ecology

Water emerges. Under
the shower in Lisbon

the spout serenades
my body, it pulsates

a sprawling spring.
Gushing, I close

my eyes & I am
stuck, in the sea,

lopsided against
the rushing waves.

*He died
in the water, he couldn't swim.*

Same day I see a headline
of a Sudanese teenager

washed up on the shores of
Calais. To drown. *He died*

*in the water, he couldn't
swim.* My mother tells me of a boat

capsized in Cox's Bazar,
deep ecology.

She fears water, so I do, too.
Traumatic retention, but have I drowned?

I cannot recall. But I do call Pacha Mama, a merciful beast,
we don't deserve you.

He died in the water, he couldn't swim.
The wildness usurped him, engulfing him cold.

Mama, take what is yours,
we are borne of you, seventy percent.

The tides call us, an *adhaan*.
I am a wave, take me, I pray.

Mother, make me strong.
If you want my body, I won't fight.

I'll die in the water, too.
I'll swim   *to you*.

Connecting With The Earth Is The Antidote To Oppression

Connecting with the Earth is the antidote to depression.

Fariha Róisín

Fear, I Give You Back

For Joy Harjo

Carried on me like
a camel's hump
I've held you close
a forsaken biblical artifact.

It is a learned thing, fear.
To be in, all consumed
my sweet, gentle nature
usurped by the foreign thud.

Oh fear, you
have me in your grip again,
peeling me into a sunburn
slightly you cut, you stab.

You repeat after me:
"You are worthless. You are nothing."
A comedic villain,
rubbing salt at my existence,

making me irritable, small.
Your voice so ancient I see
nanu in your gaze, I see
ammu's eyes, lecherous, wounded.

Fear, a word by any other name,
would sound as primordial
& yet human evolution relies
on its collapse.

To fear or not to fear? That is the
question—whether 'tis nobler in
the mind to suffer from it,
the capitalistic design that arrows

outrageous fortune, & to take &
take, for a hypothetical scarcity,
to steal, to pillage, to bear arms
to seas, to lands,

to fear the unknown,
than to accept the devices of our own inhumanity.
To accept & surrender,
instead of probing

the darkness, to fear.
Like some boring
small-minded twat.
Fear, I release you. To the wind,

like a devil's mantra, I turn my
ear away from you. I'm done
with this self-erosion,
your weak alarms.

Instead I breathe the sun,
I breathe in light, God's sanctuary
I release myself,
be gone now.

Vesuvius

"You gotta leave yesterday where it is, behind you.
Look forward, even if it's blurry."
—Narcy in a text, 9/23/2020

Overflowing,
ain't it quaint
to know what's coming
& to do it anyway?
To look a thief in its gloom
& let that motherfucker steal
from your sweet cherished home
anyway?

Don't be surprised by
the current of human
dishonesty,
a stream of lurking
dissatisfaction. Were we built
to be better?
What compulsion
against truth?

Most of human civilization
admits it likes drama. Reality TV
fills a hole,
a heart-sized lacuna.
Impoverishment of the mind
affects the soul 2 + 2 = 4.

Do I still have to say it?
Come on now, climate change.
I've only been telling you since
preschool. Too bad you
didn't Greta Thunberg yourself
out earlier.

We're trying over here,
those of us who can see the charts,
the blinding spectacle of historical &
planetary reckoning.
She's done with us, the sons of
Cain & Abel. *Who saveth us now?*
No one's going to Mars!

You fuckers wanted this land so much
for *this*? For a moment, a split
singular moment of bad sex,
gout, unsatisfying debauchery,
aging like a giant Cheeto,
no soul, & an everlasting death
in the pits of Dante's hell?
Ya gon get it, like Thatcher did.

Damn it must be dark
being that shortsighted.
A millenia who?
I'm just fucking around.
But *Die. Die. Die. You lonely heathens.*
There's work to repair

Babylon failed us all,
but that castle from Thor is waiting
or who knows, utopia.

Fariha Róisín

Fuck the Police

For the lineage, after Sean Bonney

For every stinging baton
loose like a pole,
a lost swinging dick.
For every coked-out,
misplaced bravado
that never learned the beauty
& power behind a human body.
For the sadistic pleasure,
the harm of the state,
soiled in the veins of the true &
only agitator.

For the blasting sirens, glazed
eyes, bulky, ugly NYPD regalia like a dollar store
costume that wreaks havoc on Halloween.
For the scarab-cursed eyes
sockets like rotting bloom
in the loins of Pharaoh's tomb.
For the lives, dead & taken
for the lack of serving & protecting
for every uniformed officer who slammed the body of someone I love
for every forlorn piss-smelling Klan member disguised
for the historic dissolution, rape, or hidden murder
for your wives
for your partners that hold you as you fail them
for your failure to comprehend
punishment was never the answer.

To transform the masses
you have to humanize them first.

Go on now:

abolish the cop
in   your   head
&
in   your   heart.

What Is a Border?

Who does a border, border?
& what does a border do?

Who gains from a border, *you?*

I didn't realize a border
that bordered   the border
          would really
border   me.

I am borderless.   .

          You see,
          I am not small.

I am not made out of limitations.

          I am free.

To the New, New

For Disha Ravi

The sun, like a gorgeous undulating force
dances past the shadows lurking across
the planes. A spark of lightning
maroons the distance, the territories illustrious
moon gilded, guides. Edges shaped, my heart's
interior has spoken, ten of cups,
the cycle of life, the circuitous touchdown of
dear universe's mouth pours over
to hear you sing, to believe in love again.
We have come unknown, unsung,
but we are believers
in utopia, in paradise, in the bright dawn
that seeks to field the truth, through
the rapture of the storm.
Bring the lark, to hear her
speak, we are moving to the future,
we've known like an oracle, a peak.
Come, come, come hear her hum
the past rhymes, the cursive of the stars.
The planet's rind is calling, she's coming
out of hiding, she's bringing new demands.
The world tilts in transformation, the wisdom
bears our command.
Holding our hearts out, we listen, we
understand, we pray, for a new
day, a better day, for the sun's
mysterious compassion.

From A to X

For John Berger, for Etel Adnan

Pyramid-shaped lilacs, freshly agile, a bee-stung breeze, hissing of
caramel, I hear the tender gallop of the rain. Springtime in New
York with such a dewy glow. The trees succulent like a melon rind.
Absolutely, I am taken, absolutely. The sun ripens as my body, brown,
brown body, this body, sings. I temper with a cool undulating rhythm,
floating with a raspberry in my mouth. There's nothing like the
feeling of lying bare-backed grass on my stomach. The natural world
meets me where humans cannot.

How to Hone Your Intuition

The globe lamp orbits like an alien light beam. Blood smells like
blood on this day of revolution. Solstice brings no resolution, only
might to bring the Empire down. Howling under American drones
I pluck my finger up like a joystick. The state knows nothing of why
or how the tower falls. The Tarot tells us to nurse our wounds, lick
the cuts that Capitalism has borne, here. Burn it down at Freedom's
gate. Not a day goes by that I don't see you through the dulcet smoke.
You're screaming for salvation. Through your muzzled mouth I can
hear you. *Burn it all down & start again,* you say. *With something better—
believe in better,* you tell me.

Wounds to Instincts

*"The capitalist accumulation of white supremacy has enriched
itself off the blood of our countries. We cannot forget this."*
—Cathy Park Hong

Rosewater drenched,
orange blossom
& pistachios lick
across the ashes,
          the seeds, a
passion of change, scripture
announced.
Drenched in syrupy honey,
ding ding goes the sound of
revolution.
Pashtun prints that run mercy
Allah in the cursive of the print.
Geometry, like a
mountain, streams rushing
through us   past us
to turn our fates around.
Aye, white man,
skinny, leering
like a twig found
on the heath,
cliff.   You tried to burn
us to the ground,
shouting Witch! Shouting
Musulman! Muslamic! Islamic!

Weird no occupying soldier
ever tells themselves to go back home . . .

It quakes, it purrs,
I feel the rupture, rapturously
radiating right through me,
a bullet wound. Herodotus
knew to tell a story, you had to
respect it first.

My body is a vessel
that carries truth, like a story,
God, please let me
speak the truth.
Tick, tick, boom.
I hear her, I hear
her buzzing.
What do
they say about
keeping us locked,
tight & sound?
Justice is coming,
justice is coming,
here here,   we said
it'd come.

Under Orion

I've had phlegm stuck
between my tonsils,
under my chest,
like a deep cavern,
of longing, of lust.
This breath of mine
was taken
by the last cry
of my grandmother
who was said to occupy,
linger,
alongside me
until a healer turned her
toward the light
& said, "Go."
The phlegm   lodged
inside me
that sap-like sickness,
as present as a prayer.
Painful, ugly, a harrowing ordeal.
My body stranded
between "self-actualization"
& "norms."
How do you tell a body to trust itself?
There's nothing morose here, but death.
The macabre slicks out like a phantom's reach
& I can't help but look at what is dark
& say *aha,*
I see you now.

My body is just a body.
Lingering between worlds & monsters.
For the first time,
the phlegm has dissipated.
No longer a runny-nosed remnant
of how my physical self fails me,
I fail no one anymore.
I am bright,
tall like a mountain I've learned to climb.
I long for the Himalayas,
for a solitude that will take me
where I will be with you, God.
I only wish to find you in everything,
& these days
you're in the air of every arrival.
Finding embodiment has meant
finding you
in this body
that holds it all.
Miraculous, how chronic pain
is both the wound & the opening.
Speaking out & for us,
never against,
only toward.
As I write this, I want to cry
because nothing feels truer
than finding peace in myself.
As I am, *as I am.*
Life in all its forms,
the mercy in its wake.

How the creek gestures
water down the passages
of cement that dry the land,
molding the path ahead.
Holding it for all of us.
I am the Earth, the fire & the wet mud.
I am Diana, I am the sword.
A wolf has been emerging in my dreams.
She is me; gray-haired & blue.
I look like my mother.
There's still grief in that.
Grief because when I sigh,
I exhale her.
Blood of my blood, made in her image.
The mother that births,
then denies,
then discards.
Medusa, a plight.
I don't cry
with others anymore,
now I counsel myself.

But the wolf *hears* me,
    she lets me sing.

Survival Takes a Wild Imagination

"Don't put your shoe on my shoulder & call it a hand."
—Tongo Eisen-Martin, *Heaven Is All Goodbyes*

Yes, I'm changing,
yes, I've changed.

Nothing rings
truer than
blazing through
the bright white
streak of
eucalyptus
fire we decided
to call life.

The feeling
of peeling
my skin
with a razor.
Red blood clots
pouring in monstrous
clumps, frozen,
blinded
by the brightness.
This is life, this is life
but we go on.

I've not had a good life.
I hoped that would give me
some sweet sympathy
from my peers & loved ones
or at the very least some
adulthood ease, *but*
God tests those
he loves the most,
they say.

I believe it.
Finally overcome
by divine love,
yet ease
is never immediate.
It takes time to quiet
the mind. To still
the restless soul.

To be human
is to be an unpeeled lychee,
fleshy, wet,
gelatinous, like an eyeball,
exposed. Some of us have more
wounds while others look at us
& think we act crazy when we
speak. How dare we use words
to express the pain, why not
stay silent? Grumpy?
Self-hating? Mean-spirited?

Why choose
evolution when you could
also not? They hate you
for trying. For insisting
& defending a humanity
they deny you.

The thing is, no one
will ever tell you
straight. So many will redirect
you away from yourself.
Even those
who say they love you won't
know what it means to not have
a home, to lose a parent who
betrayed you.
But, I promise, *baby*,
choose yourself. Resist
the fake love. Make sure
you remember a feeling of bliss.
Carry it with you at all times
in your mind's eye.

Don't allow
others to invalidate what you know.
Love what holds you, your body, in place.
Move toward love you don't
have to ask for, to those kindred souls
who remind you
you're easy to love.

Find God in every sweet pore,
bone, & inch of hair. Look at yourself
& feel it. You're free.
Forgive them, now yourself.

You're free.

Consequence of Hunger

When I think about you,
my body becomes a violin string
struck, vibrating like a shattering
plate, ringing like a whistle.

To be in a state of hunger
is to feel helpless.
God Almighty brought the cool
limeade to my lips

the steely glass reverberating on
my tongue
but then told me, *wait.*
My name means joy but when have I felt it?

I've spent my whole life in
the waiting room, a cluster of ants
spiraling across my legs.
I was recently told I was

like honey,
smooth, tasty,
but *sticky*, hard to remove,
like hunger. Impertinent, unruly.

We shut us down
with interrogating insults, the amount of shots fired
I've lost count.
But, I am no longer small for anyone.

No longer trapped like a dead balloon,
I resurrect myself, Joan of Arc,
from those who don't care to listen
when you speak about pain, not glory.

So many people have failed me,
but, look at me, I'm still here.
Body to moon; Earth to esophagus,

no matter how hard I tried

to shave myself to a tiny dismissive speck
of dust. Erasing my hips, to my ass,
carving myself like clay. I'm still here,
looking at you.

An Incantation

i.

I'm turning back to the girl
made out of soil & bones.
I'm seeing my hips move sensuously

as I parade by my newly bought
full-length mirror, tall, like a glass
of milk.

Fraught with the vision I had of me, I remember
the version I was forced to forget, *La Loba*,
she pines, sinking teeth into grief.

This is the melody that unites me soul to body,
I'm not yours to be made, I'm mine
to discover.

Accommodating no fool, no
commiserating audience,
I can't be bought, I only just got my freedom back!

*Everyone wants to be me but nobody wants to be
me.* It's all questions &
projections & no concerns of the heart.

Why engage with the heartless? Trendsetters
don't give a fuck about you. Janet Mock
once told me the girls who care the most

are the ones that don't need anything *<from you>*.
Survival is not for the weak, sometimes
you gotta kick so hard you break your leg—

see, survival is learning how to kick the door down
with a broken, rickety leg.
When you complain, they'll say,

Come on now, at least you're alive! Never once
acknowledging, not only have they never broken their leg,
but the door was wide open by the time they got around.

Survival is remembering yourself.
No matter how well-meaning those
who want to convince you out of being you are . . .

But no one who loves you will tell
you to forget. *Pay attention* to those who ask you
to forgo your own sanity for theirs.

Your own needs were never a burden,
sweetie. You were born into a world
of scarcity. But I'm here, & I commiserate.

I hide in plain sight. That's what it's like
to understand people. To watch their actions
as they s p e a k in words they claim are theirs,

but I see through the façade, ashes to ashes.
Sin is so obvious, I find it embarrassing that
so many succumb.

But I'm not a moralizer, I'm too sympathetic.
I forgive those who have exploited me, for the
quaint satisfaction of momentary power.

But I gave you it, I handed over the whip—
now you're mad I claimed my sovereignty? Please.
I'm taking it back, but it was always mine to take.

This is an ancient me,
I'm remembering what the women
from my lands were like before, *before*.

I was always free, always in charge.
But she made me think I was stunted,
frozen in the back seat.

I keep having a flashback.
Dad's taking us through the woods, ma's in the front.
We get to a lake, he wants to show us a trick,

he begins to back the car toward the water,
& a rush emerges. Ma is screaming but I'm stunned
by the water, by the closeness of death.

Even then, I knew it was a threat.
It didn't work, she jousted & won &
decided to kill us instead.

We're the dead children, apu & I. We're the lost ones
from broken parents, & mysterious patterns
of hy(i)ste(o)rical violence.

What do I say to him now? *You failed me,*
but I love you. Forgiveness is holding the
multiplicity.

I want to give her my steaming hot heart & say:
mend this with me. But she can't even hold her own
with tenderness. Like a bolt, she's shut to softness.

Prageeta Sharma says: "Closure
isn't closure but openings." Thank you, I tell ma
in my silence, *I am who I am because of you.*

ii.

I'm feeling the rain on my skin,
the petrichor scent like slight coriander
& remembering heart to thunder

that I am in control of my life.
I've already survived.
I don't need to run anymore.

In my dreams you hold my hand
& I am not afraid. In my dreams
you love me like a mum oughta.

I wish I had you. The grief feels
suffocating. Another Mother's Day
past & I sit, alone, anticipating violence.

I hate that's what's left of this
former life. I hate that I speak to you in riddles,
through poems.

Your *kabitha* is my *kabitha*. My heart is yours, too,
but I am not yours to own,
& I never will be.

When you're ready, I'll meet you there. In the foothills of the
Himalayas. The snow, like a crust across the surface of the Earth,
I'll see you. Across the lands of Kushtia. The porous hinterland.

I'll pray for your redemption, through the eucalyptus trees,
I'll lay you to rest in the dirt, in the waters of Pabna,
I'll pray to Allah & Oshun, for you, ma. I'll never stop.

I want your peace,
& I want mine,
too.

In the darkness, I see you & I understand you.
Motherhood isn't for everyone.
These days, I ask if it's even for me.

You readied me for an apocalypse, ma.
When you've never had stability, inheriting
a dying planet is easier, gentler.

I've always been on the cusp of
death. The faintness tastes like misery,
an aspartame sweet.

When you never had much
to lose, the betrayal is less pungent.
You instilled a survivor, ma, you made me brave.

I can't remember what you look like
anymore. The memory of your face is too painful
but each day has its own consolation.

Is it weird that, time after time,
I'd choose this life again? This majestic
clarity that heartbreak brings.

I love myself for committing to this
healing, for embracing it, for allowing
it to cleanse me. For not resisting anymore.

I'm here, both eyes open wide,
seeing truth is naming it as well.
I'm doing it for the both of us,

two peas in a pod, my karma is tied to
yours, ma. Two sides of the same coin,
lightness meets darkness, innocent by design.

I'll love you forever,
my first unattainable love,
I'll see you on the horizon

of the new dawn.
I'm praying to meet you there,
when the sun falls sharp

on the axis of our hearts, aligning
with the moon. With the fire vested
in me, I'm arriving.

Glossary

Aligarh – a prominent public Muslim university

samskara – mental impressions, recollections, or psychological imprints

Amar sonar Bangla – the Bangladeshi national anthem, translates to "My Golden Bengal"

manoosh ki bolbe – "What will people say?" in Bangla

Hanuman – the Hindu God and divine companion of the God Rama

Cox's Bazar – a beautiful city and fishing port in southeastern Bangladesh

nafs – according to the Sufi philosophies, the nafs in their unrefined "ego" state, which is considered to be the lowest dimension of a person's inward existence, their basest selves

datura – a Sanskrit word to mean "thorn-apple" and was given to the plant because of its psychoactive properties, as well as its fatal nature

adhaan – the Arabic word for "call to prayer" in Islam

La Loba – literally, she-wolf; however, La Loba (when capitalized) is the name of a mythical woman from the Pueblo people. The myth has been popularized by Clarissa Pinkola Estés in her book *Women Who Run with the Wolves*.

kabitha – the word "poem" in Bangla

Acknowledgments

I'd like to thank God and the Earth for the guidance and fortitude they have both granted me in this lifetime.

I'd like to thank Grandmother and all the medicines that have allowed me to come back to myself. For the natural world's brilliance and ardent resolution.

I'd like to thank my ancestors on both sides for guiding me here, for loving me eternally.

I'd like to thank my parents for creating and honoring me as best they could and can.

I'd like to thank my father, in particular, for being the coolest dad I could have asked for, and for being a man I admire. Thank you for listening even when you don't understand, thank you for paying attention to my boundaries when I say no. Thank you for trying even when you had no resources. Thank you for wanting to be in my life. Thank you for healing toward me. Thank you for accepting me.

I'd like to thank my sister for being an inspiration in everything I do. For being a force and a powerhouse in her own right. Thank you for making me a punk and a weirdo. Even if you don't know it, I owe so much of this to you.

I'd like to thank the Earth and Water defenders across the planet that are uniting and fighting for the Earth and her inhabitants—for the four-legged creatures, insects, and trees, for the hummingbirds and snakes and wolves and precious deer. Thank you for teaching me who I am. Thank you for showing me about sacred reciprocity. Thank you for teaching me how to listen.

I'd like to thank my friends who pay close attention and nurture me and are patient with me, who show me compassion for my roving moods and endless emotion. Thank you to my friends who can hold my darkness and love me through the storm.

I'd like to thank my readers, new and old. I'd like to thank those who have been following my work since Two Brown Girls, who have read every book and who call me their favorite writer . . . thank you. I am endlessly grateful for you.

I'd like to thank other child sexual abuse survivors for your courage, for your radiance, for your beautiful humanity. I am with you, I love you, and I will fight for the respect we deserve until the end of time.

I'd like to thank everyone that's believed in me and not stood in my way. Blessings be to those of you who have seen my power and respected me through the process.

Thank you to my editors Patty Rice and Danys Mares and the whole team at Andrews McMeel; it has been an honor to work with you. Thank you to Tarfia Faizullah who edited this book and helped me get to its core; I admire you so much and I'm thankful for your ear and heart on these pages. Thank you to Arsh Raziuddin for under-standing what this book symbolizes and for making my favorite cover of any book yet. I am so grateful to all of you.

I'd like to thank Rami for being a gift that unravels daily.

Index

Index

Index

About the Author

Fariha Róisín is a multidisciplinary artist, born in Ontario, Canada. She was raised in Sydney, Australia, and is based in Los Angeles. As a Muslim, queer Bangladeshi, she is interested in the margins, in liminality, otherness, and the mercurial nature of being. Her work has pioneered a refreshing and renewed conversation about wellness, contemporary Islam, and queer identities, and has been featured in the *New York Times*, *Al Jazeera*, the *Guardian*, and *Vogue*. She is the author of the poetry collection *How to Cure a Ghost* (2019) as well as the novel *Like a Bird* (2020) and memoir *Who Is Wellness For?* (2022). This is her second book of poetry.

Andrews McMeel Publishing
a division of Andrews McMeel Universal
1130 Walnut Street, Kansas City, Missouri 64106

www.andrewsmcmeel.com

23 24 25 26 27 MCN 10 9 8 7 6 5 4 3 2 1

ISBN: 978-1-5248-7822-1

Library of Congress Control Number: 2023935464

Editor: Patty Rice
Art Director: Julie Barnes
Designer: Tiffany Meairs
Production Editor: Brianna Westervelt
Production Manager: Shona Burns

Cover design by Arsh Raziuddin

ATTENTION: SCHOOLS AND BUSINESSES

Andrews McMeel books are available at quantity discounts
with bulk purchase for educational, business, or sales promotional use.
For information, please e-mail the Andrews McMeel Publishing
Special Sales Department: sales@amuniversal.com.